18
Hearts

Poetry by
Renato Sa

Cover Art Copyright © 2023 by Daniel Sansão
Cover Photo Copyright © 2023 by NordWood Themes on Unsplash
Edited by Rachel Koontz

1st Edition | 01
Hardcover ISBN: 979-8-9890939-8-4

First Published November 2023

For inquiries and bulk orders, please email:
indieearthbooks@gmail.com

Printed in the United States of America   1 2 3 4 5 6 7 8 9

Available in Paperback:
979-8-9890939-5-3

Indie Earth Publishing Inc.
| Miami, FL |

www.indieearthbooks.com

INDIE EARTH

18 Hearts

Renato Sa

For Jay and Gabriel

Table of Contents

Introduction

It was the same thing every day at the school cafeteria: a ham and cheese sandwich and a Mineirinho, a local soda. I actually didn't like it much, but they didn't sell Coca-Cola.

Then, one day, to my surprise, the guy at the counter said:

"We don't have Mineirinho."

I panicked. What would I drink during recess? I hesitated. I didn't know what to order. The line was long, the kids were hungry, I had to make a decision. Quickly!

"What else do you have?" I asked, trying to sound mature at the prime of my 8-year-old life.

"We have Pepsi."

Pepsi? Damn. I had heard of it. Should I order one? Should I get water only?

The kids around me were anxious. It had been two minutes already in that dilemma, standing in line trying to decide. Renato! Make up your mind!

"Sure, I'll have a Pepsi," I said.

My left hand was now hot feeling the heat of the sandwich through the napkin. Right one was cold, carrying that strange black liquid in a glass bottle.

I sat down. Took a bite of the sandwich. Check. It tasted the same. Time for a nervous sip. Let's see how this Pepsi thing tastes...

OMG! I thought, waaaaay before 'OMG' was an expression. Pepsi tastes JUST like Coke! It was one of the biggest revelations of my childhood– up until that point, at least. And I HAD to tell everyone!

I finished my sandwich and went around approaching all my friends. I don't recall how many kids I told: "Did you know Pepsi tastes just like Coke? Have you ever tried Pepsi? OMG, Pepsi is so good!"

———

This dramatic story from my childhood illustrates something very important to me: the need to communicate. Expressing myself, my feelings, and opinions has always been part of my personality.

And it's all on my face anyway. If I'm happy or sad, excited or depressed, you'll see it right away. Poker face? Can't do it. If I have a royal flush in my hands, you'll know. Don't bet.

I'm definitely a new soul. I trust people. I laugh at silly jokes. I cry with soap operas. And I honestly can't believe I'm almost half-a-century-old.

Words have always been my good friends. For a natural communicator who can't draw a straight line, vowels and consonants are a powerful ally. No wonder I decided to work with them every day. As a Journalist, I knew I'd be writing words for a living. Not necessarily the ones I wanted, but it wasn't bad. Moving to a country that doesn't speak my language put a premature end to my work in journalism, but that's another story.

All of this to say that this — my love of words — is the reason you have this book in your hands right now, and I appreciate it so much that you have read it up to this point.

Publishing my first book is a dream come true.

———

What you'll read here is not journalism. It's not news. It's poetry.

Here, you'll find the kid that needed to communicate.

The responsible professional that uses words to pay the bills.

The attentive father who loves his kids more than anything else.

The passionate lover who can fall in love with songs and smiles.

The poet who believes that poetry is not only prose in stanzas.

In addition to it all, you'll find many distinct versions of me here. Versions that don't even exist, brief thoughts, random feelings. Desires. Dreams. Different ways I absorb, feel, and live my poetic reality.

Welcome to my wor(l)ds. Come in and make yourself at home.

About this book

Yes, art is art. There's no need to explain. However, I've discovered through my life that, when you learn about what an artist really meant when creating that painting, movie, poem, etc., that can help you better comprehend their (he)art.

So, I've decided to give you a hand.

This book is the result of the last six years of my life. When I launched Poetic Frames on Instagram back in 2017 — thanks, Rafa! — I was going through a professional crisis. Going back to poetry was very therapeutic — and it has been ever since. I used to write poetry as a kid and went through a long time away from it. It's great to be back.

Organizing poems is almost impossible. They come in different shapes and sizes and represent unique poetic phases of my life (granted, a "poetic phase" may only last a few hours). So, I've decided to divide them into, well, shapes and sizes.

Part I of this book has the more traditional poems. When I say "traditional," I mean regular verses and stanzas. My poems are not perfectly metered, as formal poetic rules would require.

Read Part II when you don't have much time to spare. Need a quick shot of poetry and beauty in your day? Turn to this section of the book. Go for it. These short poems are a hit on Instagram because they are easy to digest.

Part III is — maybe — my favorite. Here I try to go beyond words and poetry and play with their shapes. I've always been a fan of concrete poetry, and this is my best attempt at it.

And finally, regarding the title: "18 Hearts." This is the poem that opens the book, but it is also more than that. Some people have asked me the question over the years: "What's 18 hearts?"

Ever since I came back to writing poetry, I have also begun to understand what really matters to me. Today, I try to downsize my life and much as I can, carefully selecting the actual stuff that surrounds me. At the end of the day, I really don't need much more than a simple home, food, and some clothes to live.

Nonetheless, I need many, many hearts to embrace, to absorb and experience this life to the fullest — and to love my friends, family, and lovers as much as I can.

"But why 18?"

Eighteen is not only a big number. It was also the day my brother, my sister and I were born. And they are always with me.

Part I: Dive

i don't need much

three shirts
couple of shorts
a pair of sandals

two cups
spoon, fork, knife
a plate

a roof
a bed
18 hearts

to adjust the course
and lose track

to keep it together
and release my demons

to pick up the pieces
and stay at peace

i write to right my wrongs
to come back to where i belong

it feels like an endless meadow
spreading in a steady flow
sliding, slow
creeping as vines

unfolding as i conquer
yet surrender at the same time
as a lace, a flawless embrace
a perfect wrap of senses

as a knot, with no end in sight
a complete mess of souls
entwined, we unwind
i do love

hugging us

i'm not a poet

i just recycle emotions
by rearranging characters

a digital surgeon of sorts
sorting mixed feelings

i extract sounds here
implant rhymes there

stitching ruptures only
to heal my own self

a hammock is a nest
a place to rock
a place to rest

a no-place in fact
no thinking/no planning
no sweat

here i breathe
i gaze
i nothing

i morph
& merge
into you

a hammock
my love
is a poetry bed

have always wondered
where love goes
after leaving
one's heart

maybe it goes up
straight to heaven
back to a huge
beautiful cloud

perhaps it goes down
nonstop to hell
back to the core
in the center of the world

truth is that love
doesn't go anywhere
it just stays in one's soul
ready to be born again

my senses are now heightened
to absorb every grain of you

life is muted and beautifully blurred
in this meditative state

comprehending objects and dialogues
requires focus and faith

inside this box shaped like your body
i can only feel your overwhelming presence

you breathe inside me

our recipe

4 l eggs
butt er
a cup of silk
a splash of flower
a bit of mating power

there's nothing like
the love we bake

some write so that
people can follow

they want followers

i write so that
people can flow

i want flowers

GPS

select location:
completely lost

enter destination:
inside your hug

searching...
searching...
searching...

destination not found
review the location and try again

no need to worry
whatever happens
i'll always have

~~you~~
the ocean
the beatles
häagen-dazs dulce de leche

i hide behind
silent notes

i escape to an
state of awe

i breathe through
peaceful fields

i am the moment
i blend with time

i am whole
with poetry

saudade is not a verb
for it doesn't move

it is a solid noun
here to stay

more than feeling
the absence

it's craving
the presence

saudade is the love
that remains

if only verses could be
more than lines
words not just rhymes

a mediocre life
would be more divine
simple moments, sublime

if only we could go back
to brighter times
you'd be mine again

my valentine

i still remember
when we met

a million words
ago

it was love
at first rhyme

sun	in scorpio
mercury	in scorpio
venus	in scorpio
mars	in scorpio
heart	in turmoil

you know
between
you and me

you're the best
of both
words

dear child,

life can be hard
sometimes

please be dareful
out there

wish

roam through
enchanted hearts
weightless

drift away
in a current
of no regrets

get lost
entwined with
good souls

curl my fears
as night falls
sleep in the clouds

a piece of the sun
a bite of the wind

wine for the soul
music for the heart

a deep breath
loaded with peace

some days life just
flows through you

mercifully

i'm always gone
from the place
where i am

though i thought
i was now here
i am nowhere

today i finally
found myself
and want to stay

it is time
to come back to
where i will be

me

like a cancer
that spreads but won't kill
some kind of blindness
that makes you see more every day

a type of dementia
that highlights your memories
a rare condition
that makes your heart quiver

i gave up fighting
this chronic illness
and learned to survive
with severe missingness

as i walk through
this winding road
i become more forgiving
with the steps i take

i'm the travel
and the traveler
the beginning
and the journey's end

departing and arriving
to and from me
the ultimate, most beautiful
destination

i envy the symmetric brains
and their cartesian minds

the ability to be precise
never looking behind

poor me, stumbling
between the lines

trying to find my way
always undefined

lost in a maze of doubts
poorly rhymed

i observe the chaos
i absorb madness

i inhale tension

i follow the wind's direction
i swallow thunderstorms

i digest disasters

i operate in the dark
i obturate demons

i exhale poetry

call it a trick, a hidden card,
magic, if you will

when the rain goes from
graceful to unpredictable

and the air is so heavy you can
touch it with your thoughts

when you're hit by life so hard you feel
endless and minuscule at the same time

i pull you from my spiritual pocket
to protect me with thick layers of hope

though faded and stained, your glow
cuts through reality like a divine razor

offering a subtle, kind purpose just
enough to bring me back to surface

and let me breathe again

these words were hidden yesterday
they respect me
they don't come in extreme sadness

they wait to be written
as they simmer
right under my skin

they perceive
they absorb
the violence of ghosts

they are born infected
loaded with vehemence
they keep me company

the day after

it was great seeing you next week
now i crave yesterday's romance
i miss you when you're here
i feel you without knowing you

i keep wanting you
way before
way beyond
logic and time

for you have
never been
never will
you simply are

infinite

we have never met
many times before

never talked
in various occasions

never fallen in love
in countless moments

we always
almost

baby, we are definitely
meant to be

away

poetry should be put in its own
'love' category
along with kindness
care and passion

as a noun, as a verb
by itself
way beyond its original
literary work meaning

"he treats her with so much poetry"
"she poetried him the moment she saw him"

for a poem is more
than words in a verse
it's love
condensed in stanzas

a critical toxin in my veins
dopamine for the soul
adrenaline for the pulse
you're an impulse

an endorphin
oxytocin
my life support
my last resort

a lifeline
to my vital signs
my core and my spine
my one and only

[undefined]

there was a meadow, green, vast
it was cloudy and i wanted to go inside
but i stayed out a bit longer

contemplating
feeling that repeated yet
never lived before moment

you were there
frozen in that micro reality
faceless, waiting for me

the carrier
the bearer
of infinite love

i fall in love
break up and
walk away from

people
places
moments

all the time

the mere brevity of life
makes me
instantly nostalgic

i met this flower growing in the dolomites
her petals yellow
she invited me to lie
down by her and taste the truth

i merged with the rocks
me and soil one, same thing now
i begged her not to eat my eyes
mushroom clouds above us

can you feel the trembles
the earth pulsing below, she was curious
i now am dirt without dying
i am without being

here verbs and nouns
are the same nothings
the infinite within life
the only thing there is

some days
she wears nothing
but poetry

today she's naked
covered only
with butterflies

she stripped off her lies
and dressed herself
with rhymes

when the sounds of the backyard
embrace you with slugs
and childhood joy fades away
with the rustle of vultures

you, in this labyrinth of metaphors
alone in this agora empty of colors
a cloister of clouds
stripped of birds

remember that
between pauses and cicadas
there's so much poetry in this smooth creek
the elusive flow of life

trochaic tetrameter
double dactyls
anapestic dimeters

all poems
must be metered
they say

i measure mine
in your skin
my most beautiful prosody

halfway through
this winding road i don't want
half-baked realities

bring me
the whole cake
loaded with chaos

i want the ghosts
and the poisons
the fire and the rain

i want life full
of uncertainties
undivided

there are really
no cycles
no beginnings
no ends

life just is

but i keep inventing
stories through my
poetic eyes
because

life just is
          not enough

i like small places
tiny rooms and spaces

for i am so vast
inside already

i am an ocean of sorrows
an endless field of morals

i am a garden of feelings
a hoarder of dreams

i am more
than enough

for me

we help
        the hungry
        the poor
        the sick

but i think about
        the masses
        the crowds
        the ones

without love

i'm always whole
in my half realities

i sincerely welcome
my hidden sins

i'm completely aware
of my unknown desires

forever truthful
to my erroneous selves

i fully assume
all my irresponsibilities

i've made a decision

to go with the flow
of uncertainties

to always love blindly
at first sight

i'll stick to a routine
of unpredictable tasks

a list of pointless bullet points
aimlessly pointing nowhere

today is day one

of finding myself
centrally lost in betweenness

we woke up still floating
on the night before

lost in this colorful
morning trance

isolated
we find ourselves

we go outside
by playing inside each other

now we just need
coffee and a sunrise

i hike through the curves
of your digital skin

dancing to the sound
of your recorded voice

i lick your pores, slowly
each and every pixel

i hear your face
i smell your taste

as my senses
no longer make sense

away from you

lost as i find myself
i feel whole as a dissipate
fading but hyper aware
far away though fully there

breathless as i touch the air
silent but immersed in sounds
naked though covered in light
alive after having died

magnificent they are
these very first seconds
after making love
to us

i just keep gliding
wherever the wind goes

there are many traces
of you everywhere

for you have sprinkled
beauty all over the land

up here i only see you
when the stars align

you, the rocket
and the sky

one heaven of a ride

all she wants
is an acoustic love

with easy melodies
and calm arrangements

just a guitar
a smooth voice

& deep breaths

i miss the 80s so much
i need to police myself

so that i don't switch
my tears for fears

meantime i keep looking
for the cure to this disorder

shooting guns
& smelling roses

i'm drowning in
the dark side of time
aging a thousand verses a day

i'm a vessel to a million tears
sinking at every corner
as i fall deeply in life

stay away, stay away
i want to weep
all my secrets inside

sometimes it rains
inside the house

dark clouds occupy
rooms and minds

i can touch the air
now heavy and damp

as i navigate the tempest
eyes blind, blind

my stormy chest
has never been drier

when i'm sick
it gets sore
if i'm thirsty
it aches more

if there's a threat
a bad thought
it goes right through
my core

it's where it starts
with all my words
where it ends
when i choke

i feel life
pulsing, raw
deep down
in my throat

no weed for me, no need
no mary jane in the brain
no needle in the vein
not a grain to keep me sane

no sugar on the stream
no candy from the streets
no cheat, no sweets
no gain, no cane

no booze, no juice
to choose, no use
no need to excuse
to amuse, to confuse me

my drug of choice
is none of above
i only get high
on romantic love

those small, blue eyes
feel like childhood

your voice carries the same sincerity
and i absorb every word with care

as always, time is rare
we go back, we haven't much of it

a masked though tight hug
gives me (much needed) air

you, i swear,
still smell like teen spirit

i saw your smile today
shining on this woman's face
i bumped into—and almost grabbed
your waist at the checkout line

a few almost identical eyes
chase me around with fake gazes
along with your cologne
that smells odd given their hormones

the taste though,
the taste...
necks of total strangers
literally lickable targets

come outside
lick the drops
of moonlight

cover me
with your
perfect nights

look at the sky
our scars
are aligned

every time she writes
she divinely undefines
her multiple existences

she takes me away, this adorable
scribe as she inscribes
her poetry in me

every time she rights me
she's quite imprecise
as she artfully undescribes

meanings and feelings
in her own dictionary
of indefinitions

i walk into your
garden of sounds

at 90 memories
per hour

still licking my
jam of pearls

unchain yourself, alice
and join me in nirvana

a master in forging feelings
she plays hard with words

an expert at hiding secrets
she steals hearts and hopes

more than a robber
she's a raider

a lover like no other
an accomplice in romance

she's my muse beyond time
my unique partner in rhyme

i pile up cries
i inhale tears

i supress sighs
i curate feelings

i compartmentalize
them into soulful boxes

most die, meaningless
in my guts

some thrive
in my throat and become

breath
bile
butterflies

your poem is a midday breeze
cutting through the office-cage

a reverse defibrillator
zchunk, zchunk

pulling me out of reality
to flatline with you

come to poetic coma
let's daydream together

you don't die at once
bam
dead
you die
a little bit
every day

sometimes
you go through days
without dying
shielded
by the routine
traffic bills work

then one day you die big
strong
heavy
there's a body
a story, tears
a whole funeral inside you

but you're still there
more alive
than never

we have no colors
no brushes
no notes to dance with
no clay to shape our demons

a white paper is all there is
a canvas where we play
with small bites of sound
tiny drawings we sketch

syllables
then words
then some kind of meaning
we hope to express

otherwise
we kill
ourselves
more than any other artist

whenever you
                come
wherever you
                come
however you
                come

just bring
that loose shirt

and the wine
in your mouth

right there where

        hair ends gently
        touching shoulders
        lips northeast
        arm southwest
        freckles lightly sprinkled
        on right breast

that's where

        love is born

like mini dynamites
ready to ignite

small packs mixed with
powder and pleasure

easy to maneuver
but hard to control

he likes his lovers
short and salty

unloving is to fold back
clean up the room
pick up the pieces

it's to paint the walls gray
turn on the tv
and watch the walls

it's choosing the black umbrella
over the yellow one
not knowing the weather anyway

it's to unsing songs
deflate balloons
delete memories

unloving is not dying
though
unloving is unliving

a shot of good vibes
right through my skin
she's not just a hype
a mere scene

this fun queen
is a rare sight
often serene
sometimes obscene

quiet dynamite
always keen
almost ripe
she's so feminine

my lovely tangerine

some want to scatter
their ashes in the sea
spread themselves infinite
beyond death

i make love to the waves
floating drowning floating
flowing through their gentle pace
coming deep inside the ocean's womb

i prefer to scatter
my seeds in the sea
spreading myself infinite
beyond life

i'm completely full
of half poems

a walking draft
a rhyming zombie

i'm living in limbo
lost in lyrical hiatus

pregnant with multiple
verses and curses

waiting for a long
poetic birth

the past is right here
this present i already miss

futures are veins
spreading on the wall

vain vultures
spying on my thoughts

don't blink twice
tomorrow is almost now

seems november's here
every 12 minutes now

paul is 80
tom is 60

the queen
is dead

and yet this kid
with gray beard

keeps smiling
in the mirror

i can't draw anything
but sticks and circles
yet my drawings have
sound and meaning

they carry texture
they're colorful
painful even
at times

i draw feelings
it's called poetry

i don't want this you
with the social smile
the routine
the nice face

i want that creature
that thing you become
that transfigures
and transcends

that gets distorted
in my hands
the one that bends
the one that blends

the one
you can only recognize
and understand
through my eyes

got a ticket today for DUE
driving under emotion

apparently you can't
cry and drive

next time
when watching iñárritu

i'll be the
designated crier

i waited to read her
it was cold
i was sick

today the sun is up
the air is crisp
deep breath

i got a haircut
new shoes
a big oxygen tank

for she's a waltz
and a storm
it's time to dive into her

poetry

i miss all those years
we spent together

during that three-second kiss
i planted on your head

right in the middle
of the bookstore

i've just realized
the people i love
are made of poetry

some are poets indeed
others just don't know it
yet

love the shape of your name
first & last

the sound of your phone number
all digits

even the formatting of your email
before & after the @

so when i read write type call you
it's like you're occupying me

slow down. pause. breathe
almost
give up

...

usually (i've learned)
that's when life offers you
some compassion

waking up
with your 'likes'
is like breakfast in bed
on a lazy sunday morning

reading
your comments
is to hear you in my mouth
kiss you with my eyes

i recite
the poems you liked
slowly, to feel the poetry
echoing inside you

it's my way
to penetrate you
without even knowing
who you are

stop stop
touch these words now
try their texture
with your fingers

rub this page
against your face
feel these verses
inhale them all

they are
me
they are
mine

my feelings
condensed
decanted
imprinted

yours

i look in the mirror
and see the sky

white loose shirt
light blue shorts

matching colors
internal and external

head in the clouds
one full peace

a song is
hey, babe
a playlist is
i love you

because

there's nothing like
feeling music
through someone
you want

poetry is both
cause & consequence

the first clause & the sequence
the because & the essence

it's the applause before the dance
both the sauce & the romance

it's the pause & the stance
the poise & the presence

poetry is both
the noise & the silence

Part II: Bite

you're gone
but it's me
i miss
the most

the urge
to love you
slowly

i think
therefore
i am

i feel
therefore
i poem

it feels like
we met
a thousand
tears ago

- i have so much to tell you
- i'm all fears

women are
poetry
in flesh
and blood

here comes the pun
do, do, do
here comes the pun
and i say it's all rhyme

cowards

today
i aged
a thousand
verses

meet me
to become a word
love me
to become poetry

i always love
at first sight
better sorry
than safe

i remember when we met
a million words ago
it was love
at first rhyme

i always
sink twice
before
floating in love

fuck nudes
send me your poems
i wanna see you
naked

the heart
of a poet
it's always love
at first sigh

some days
i feel glory
for myself

the year barely started
and i've already
fallen in love
a thousand times

- so, what do you do?
- i feel.

better rage
then, sorry

she broke herself
into a million pieces
to finally find
her missing peace

and in the end
the love you didn't take
is equal to the love
you faked

Part III: Hike

iam   rigid
iam   concrete
imelt   with
s   m   i   l   e   s

iam   stiff
iam   square
irun   in
c   i   r   c   l   e   s

iam   ordered
iam   organized
ihave   many
messedupfeelings

iam   drama
iam   tragedy
ilaugh atmyown
inconsistencies

i rest in rogh corners
vlnerable bt calm
srviving long days
with no prpose

jst a mltitde
of nmb memories
random thoghts
throgh my mind

not qite a ghost
thogh not flly alive
i jst keep trying
to sstain life

withot

to day iwo keup
al l o ve r th ep lace

i lo st myh ead
c an't fi ndmy fac e

th is m issin g p e ace
i nsi sts tot ease me

i' m ap uz zle
a mill ion pie ces

a maze, a cha rad e
ass em bly i s re qui red

Daily Routine:

I. P A   C E yourself.

II. FACE   yourself.

III. EMB R AC E yourself.

a poet only wants to

t e l l   you

t ɘ a ƨ e   you

t oᴜc h   you

need
the need
the need to touch
the need to touch you
the need to touch you deeply

all of your corners and pores
all of your corners
all of you
all you
all

every time
i _____ you

there's a small
earthquake

inside my body
you,

my little pack of
tremors
tremors
tremors

a shoulder not there to lend
a letter unfinished to send

plans too broken to mend
decisions too wrong to defend

bodies too far to bend
souls too hurt to blend

poets hate
when stories _ _ _

to enthuse
to confuse

to bemuse
to abuse

to defuse
to infuse

i write poems
to amuse

there's a path. a cadence. a certain way that i depart from me. to encounter you. and graciously pour my love. i flow through peacefully. this well-known current of ours.

f   l   u   i   d

you put a dam |

i

and then
one day
they started
sleeping in

separate   bodies

an idle swing /

                  gravel roads

withered memories /

                  hazy days

inert grime /

                  vague rhymes

without love /

                  a poet is just a

ghost

longmeetingspaythebillsmakemoney
fightanxietybestrongeatwellreadmore
backstabberspointlesspresentations
behealthyofficepoliticscutbackcalories
trafficjamredlightexercisestress

i have the discipline of oldest sons
the strictness of right angles
i need the routine to ground me, though
the clock, the schedule, repetition

otherwise i drown.
in the poetic quicksand

and i'm an infinite child
time is just a rhyme
in this purple haze
in the land of words

nothing but
pure poetic
chemistry

the unique
viscosity of
your saliva

~~explains~~
exclaims
it all

at the edge
of your fingers
begins

the void
the end
the cold unknown

the entire world
before i hit
crop & delete

i grab your
nails, slippery
my last chance

to
stay
afloat

i read you between the

_ _ _ _ _ _ _ _ _ _ _

of your lips

i hike you along the

_ _ _ _ _ _ _ _ _ _ _

of your neck

i tease you below the

_ _ _ _ _ _ _ _ _ _ _

of your waist

i need you all over the

_ _ _ _ _ _ _ _ _ _ _

and places

( ) the smell of your breath
    & the taste of your skin
    (just like that, combined)
    made me love you

( ) pure love
    the purest one
    made me find those things
    simply irresistible

( ) all of the above
    in the most
    random &
    chaotic way

rocket scientist:
~~past~~
~~present~~
future

lawyer:
~~past~~
present
~~future~~

poet:
past
~~present~~
~~future~~

1 - couple of regrets
2 - many frustrations
3 - several heartbreaks
4 - one big longing
5 - a series of little agonies

otherwise
i'm happy
and boring

it's the pains
the pains that
make me interesting

when he's not playing
with (s)words
a poet has many
different (pre)occupations:

- administrator of longings
- collector of sighs
- tamer of storms
- therapist of desires
- curator of tears

I

| ooked
| icked
| iked
| oved
| ost
| ack
| ong

U

an ocean once
unpredictable

my waters are now
contained

as suppressed waves
behind a cautious dam

come open the gates
so that i can flow

through you
again

oh, the trees, i envy their
s   t   i   l   l   n   e   s   s

world going crazy and they're just
t   h   e   r   e

not suffering, not hurting, just
b   e   i   n   g

they offer me their
p   r   e   s   e   n   c   e

but i'm always ahead
in the

                              fu
                              tu
                              re

it puzzles me
how well
our bodies
fi tt ogether

when i am
deeply

in Y si O de U

i am
completely

outside   ME

you are
the love
of my
life

i just
wish you
were
here

i feel

      all
     & **one**

sometimes

How to Boost Your Low Humanity:

- Sunlight: intense shots

- Vitamin Sea: daily

- Hugs: private sessions with specialist

- Poetry: highest dosage (extra strength)

- Love: unlimited amount

verses
are my
vice

and
vice
versa

forget
  tarot
    santeria
astrology
  to really
  really
know
  someone
  kiss
them
  tongues
  don't
      lie

picture a day with
no concentration
no focus at all
just this massive blur

nothing in my mind
but one thought
dominating my soul

distracting me
non-stop
unwaveringly

your

S   E
  M   L
    I

is what

      I
   C T
 X   E
E   S

me the most

i convert feelings
into verses and
pack them together
inside tiny boxes

poems

iberian nostalgia
tropical sun
unstable childhood
cinema paradiso
+ paul's melodies
milton's voice
manoel's words
talita's heart
_____

me

u

sleeping
alone
under the moon

without

demands
seeing things from
a different perspective

feet on humid grass
automatically childhood
my personal delorean

us

is

l   os   t

in

l   us   t

18 Hearts

Renato Sa

Acknowledgments

The first kiss. The first time you fall in love. The first breakup. The first hangover. The first job. The first child. There's nothing like living something for the first time.

For my very first book, I would like to thank my mom and dad for all their love and support. It's been a long and winding and bumpy road, but it's always led me back to you both — and I'm so thankful for that.

Also, brothers and sisters — we're in this together. I'll go with you all the way to the end.

In addition to dedicating this book to you, I can't thank Jay and Gabriel enough. You are the reason for it all. I thought I knew what love was all about before you were born. I was completely, utterly wrong. Thank you, Flavia, for all the years we have spent together and for being the best mom to our children.

Thank you, Talita, for being a grandmother, a mother, a friend. A real pillar behind our family. An example of love, empathy, kindness, and charity. Thank you, Tio Padrinho, for the laughs, the terrible jokes and all the much-needed lightness I still carry with me.

My lifetime friends (in alphabetical order): Alexandre Mattoso, Carla Fraga, Gustavo Schiavone, Martin Makler. Thank you. I can't do it without you.

Special thanks to Rafa — a brother and lifetime friend — for encouraging me to launch Poetic Frames, where it all became real. Also, thanks to Ju, for always being there for me.

Thank you so much Flor Ana and Indie Earth Publishing (my amazing publisher), Rachel Koontz (my dear friend and editor), and Daniel Sansão (my friend and the best designer ever).

To all my friends, family, and lovers: thank you. If you have ever crossed my way and given me your love and/or received my love, you're still with me.

This book is for *you*.

About the Author

© Leo Sa

Renato Sa is a Brazilian poet living in Miami, Florida, and the passionate visionary behind the Instagram account @poeticframes. Born in Rio de Janeiro, he speaks and writes in English, Spanish and Portuguese and loves discovering new sounds and word combinations.

Interested in the themes of art, beauty, love, life and science, Renato believes poetry is about playing with words, their sounds, meanings, and structures. Brazilian poets Manoel de Barros, Paulo Leminski and Clarice Lispector are his biggest inspirations.

When he's not writing poetry, you can find Renato by the ocean, listening to music, and spending time with his children.

Connect with Renato:

www.instagram.com/poeticframes

About the Publisher

INDIE EARTH
PUBLISHING

Indie Earth Publishing is an independent, author-first co-publishing company based in Miami, FL, dedicated to giving authors and writers the creative freedom they deserve. Indie Earth combines the freedom of self-publishing with the support and backing of traditional publishing for poetry, fiction, and short story collections by providing a plethora of services meant to aid them in the book publishing experience. With Indie Earth Publishing, you are more than just another author, you are part of the Indie Earth creative family, making a difference one book at a time.

www.indieearthbooks.com

Instagram: @indieearthbooks

For inquiries, please email:
indieearthbooks@gmail.com

Printed in the USA
CPSIA information can be obtained
at www.ICGtesting.com
LVHW090751201223
766591LV00004B/118